Perspectives

Owning a Pet
What Should You Think About?

Series Consultant: Linda Hoyt

Flying Start
to Literacy®

Contents

Introduction

Owning a pet – is it fun or hard work?

Pets can be great company and lots of fun, but owning a pet can be hard work. It's not always easy keeping your pet healthy, happy and safe.

If you want a pet, how do you decide which pet? What are the questions you should ask?

A dog is for life ..

not just for Christmas.

Look at this poster.

What does it mean to you?

Why was it made?

What does this poster make you think about?

Speak out!

You want a pet, but what will you choose – a rabbit, a fish, a cat or a dog? Or something else?

Here, three students talk about the pet they would like to have and why.

The best pet for me would be a pet that doesn't need much attention or care. This is because I have piles of homework, piano and violin practice, and I help my sister with her homework. I also do chores for my mum. If I didn't have so much work, I would get a fish. Watching a goldfish swim would help me relax.

The pet that suits me is a dog. Why? Because a dog is a loyal, fun and friendly companion. When I was born, my mum brought home a puppy named Rosie. Sadly, this year, she passed away. Rosie could always feel my emotions – if I was happy, she was happy. And if I was sad, she was sad. That's why I'm really looking forward to getting a new puppy.

I am not a fan of pets, but my cat makes me happy. I love company, and cats love company, and I have a lot of spare time that I can spend with my cat. Cats are smart, friendly and playful, and I can teach my cat tricks. Cats are also easy to care for because they don't make much mess.

As sick as a dog

Written by Daniela Weil

Did you know that these foods are poisonous to cats and dogs?

If pets could talk, they would probably tell you that they can eat anything. But they cannot. It is your responsibility to feed them safely.

How can you protect your pet?

Chocolate

Avocados

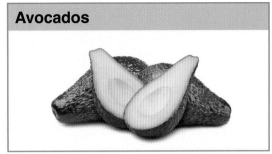

Lemons, limes and oranges

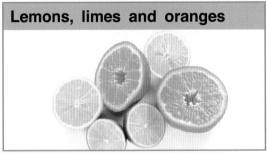

Salmon

Grapes and raisins

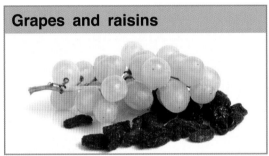

Bread that has yeast

Macadamia nuts

Sugar-free gum or lollies

Onions and garlic

Strawberries

Not everyone wants a pet

Written by Robin Cruise

Having a pet is both fun and hard work. There are many things to consider before making a pet a part of the family.

Is a puppy the right pet for Mason? What do you think?

"Mum, look!" Mason said as his mum pulled into the driveway. "It's a puppy! I've always wanted one. Can we keep him?"

Before his mother could answer, Mason hopped out of the car and hurried to the front porch.

"This puppy might belong to someone else," said his mum. "We should try to find his owner."

"Okay," said Mason. "But I'm going to call him Bud!"

Mason's mum smiled. But she didn't say a word until they got to the kitchen.

"I'll make a snack for you, Mason," she said. "And then, let's make some flyers to hand out in the neighbourhood."

"Okay," Mason said. "But I still want to keep Bud!"

When Mum put Mason's snack on the table, Bud jumped up and gobbled it down.

"Oh no!" said Mason.

Then Bud started chewing on Mason's favourite toy.

"Stop!" said Mason, as he grabbed his toy.

Bud started to whine and spin in circles.

"Mum! What's he doing?" Mason called.

But it was too late. Suddenly, there was a big puddle on the kitchen floor.

Mason's mother handed him a roll of paper towels to clean up the mess.

"Gross!" Mason muttered.

Later that day, the doorbell rang. A young girl and a man gazed at Mason and his mother.

"Hello!" the girl said. "My name is Ella, and this is my dad, Ben. Our puppy is lost. Her name is Lucy. Have you seen her?"

Ella held out a flyer with a photo of a puppy that looked just like . . . Bud! The headline read: "Puppy Lost!"

Mason held up the flyer his mother had made. "Ella," he said, "you mean . . . Bud is a girl named Lucy?"

Mason was sad to let Bud/Lucy go. But he was just eight years old, and Ella was older. He knew she could take better care of a puppy.

"We just moved in around the corner," Ella said. "Come visit Lucy anytime!"

Mason liked that idea. "Mum – let's get a puppy when I'm ten or eleven, like Ella," he said. "But maybe a turtle would be a good pet for me now!"

How to write about your opinion

State your opinion

Think about the main question in the introduction on page 4 of this book. What is your opinion?

Research

Look for other information that you need to back up your opinion.

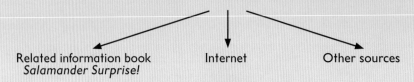

| Related information book *Salamander Surprise!* | Internet | Other sources |

Make a plan

Introduction

How will you "hook" the reader to get them interested?

Write a sentence that makes your opinion clear.

List reasons to support your opinion.

| Support your reason with examples. | Support your reason with examples. | Support your reason with examples. |

Conclusion

Write a sentence that makes your opinion clear. Leave your reader with a strong message.

Publish

Publish your writing.

Include some graphics or visual images.